Follow your dream.
Every dream has a passion,
and every passion has a destiny.
—Billy Mills

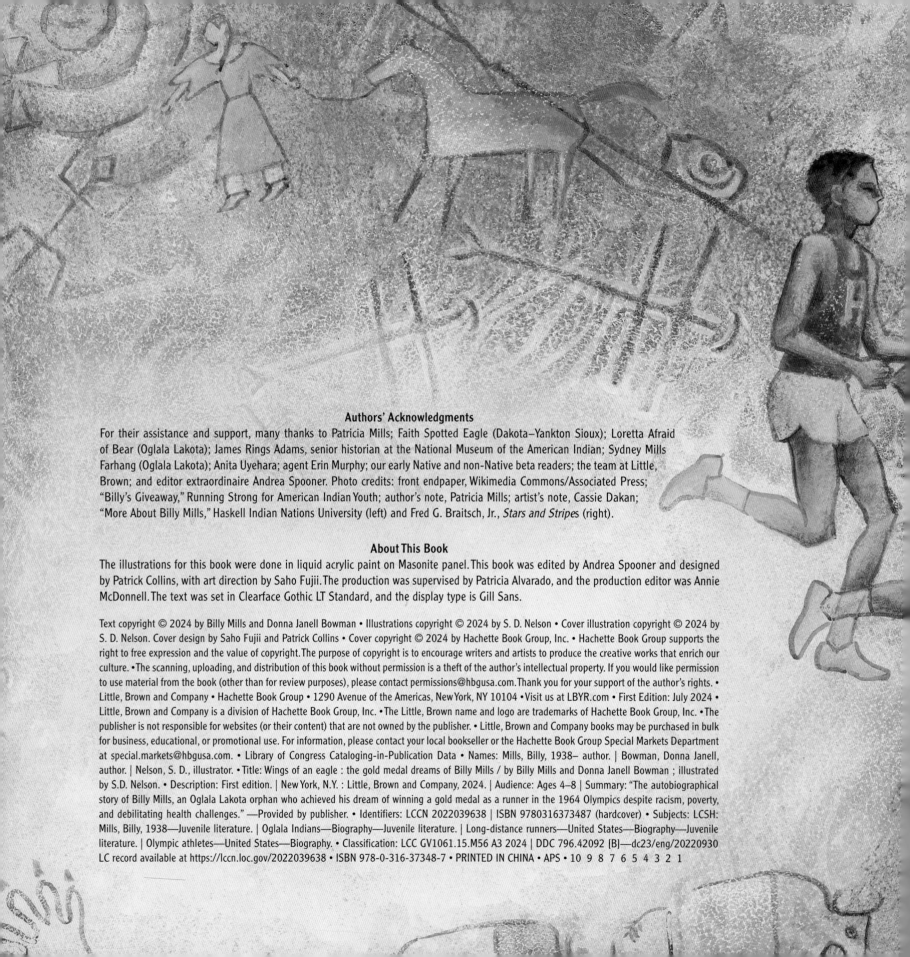

Authors' Acknowledgments

For their assistance and support, many thanks to Patricia Mills; Faith Spotted Eagle (Dakota–Yankton Sioux); Loretta Afraid of Bear (Oglala Lakota); James Rings Adams, senior historian at the National Museum of the American Indian; Sydney Mills Farhang (Oglala Lakota); Anita Uyehara; agent Erin Murphy; our early Native and non-Native beta readers; the team at Little, Brown; and editor extraordinaire Andrea Spooner. Photo credits: front endpaper, Wikimedia Commons/Associated Press; "Billy's Giveaway," Running Strong for American Indian Youth; author's note, Patricia Mills; artist's note, Cassie Dakan; "More About Billy Mills," Haskell Indian Nations University (left) and Fred G. Braitsch, Jr., *Stars and Stripe*s (right).

About This Book

The illustrations for this book were done in liquid acrylic paint on Masonite panel. This book was edited by Andrea Spooner and designed by Patrick Collins, with art direction by Saho Fujii. The production was supervised by Patricia Alvarado, and the production editor was Annie McDonnell. The text was set in Clearface Gothic LT Standard, and the display type is Gill Sans.

WINGS OF AN EAGLE

THE GOLD MEDAL DREAMS OF BILLY MILLS

By Billy Mills and Donna Janell Bowman

Art by S. D. Nelson

LB

LITTLE, BROWN AND COMPANY
New York   Boston

October 14, 1964—Olympic Stadium, Tokyo, Japan

Thirty-eight world-class runners gather on this rain-soaked track.

All eyes are on the favorites—world-record holders,

a previous gold medalist, the best of the best!

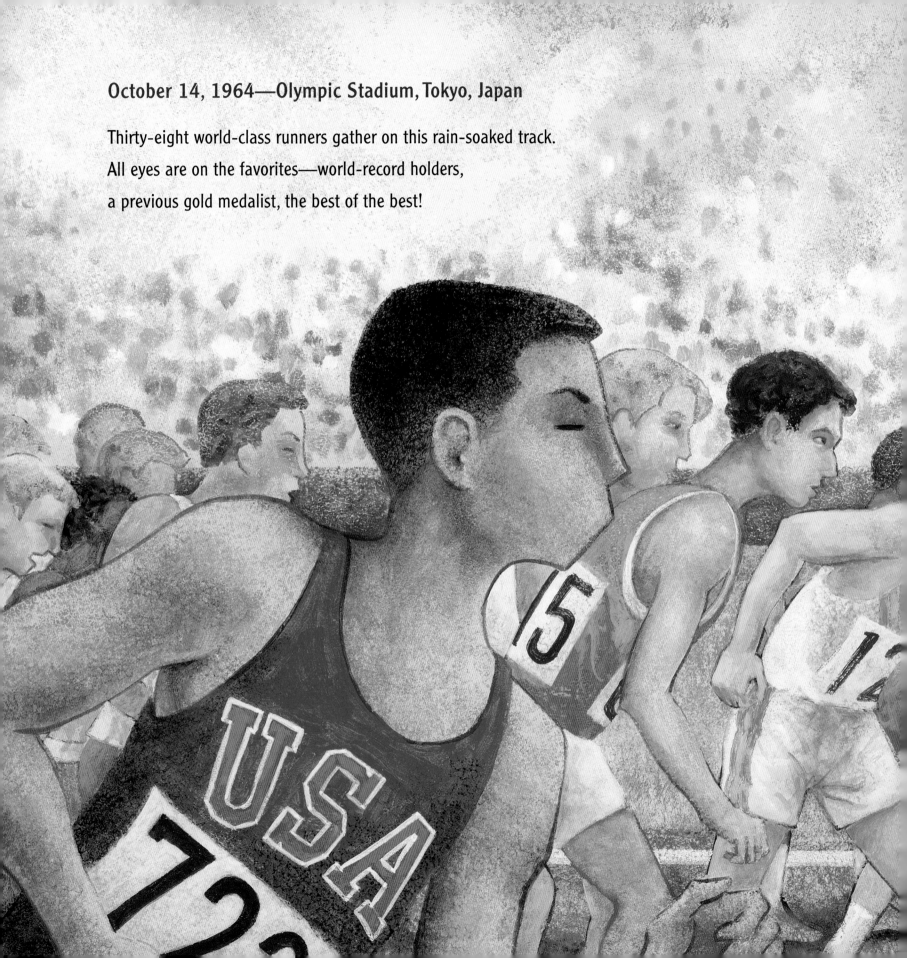

Most people don't notice me.
They don't know that I am
Oglala Lakota—Native American.
They don't know that I have wings.
But in 25 laps, 10,000 meters, 6.2 miles . . .
they will.

Bang!

My feet sprint forward but my memories rewind
to the rolling plains of Pine Ridge Reservation,
the sovereign lands of the Oglala Lakota Nation.

Our home overflows with family,

until we spill into a second house across the road—

beyond the outhouse and the water well,

surrounded by dirt-floor dwellings and poverty.

South Dakota winters bite through our secondhand clothes,

but love keeps us warm.

We are stronger together, connected by hope and culture.

At a Wacipi—a powwow—our Oglala Lakota people
join the other tribes and bands of the Great Sioux Nation
to honor our ancestors and Wakan Tanka, the Great Spirit.
Soon the ring clears for the Traditional Giveaway.
Like cupped hands, an open blanket fills with community gifts
as thanks from people with blessings and success.
I have nothing to give now,
but I wonder if someday I will have a Giveaway of my own.
We are stronger together when we give back.

It's not easy to think of others after my mother dies.

My nine-year-old feelings splinter like a nest in a storm.

My father draws a circle in the dirt.

"You have broken wings, son," he says. "Step inside the circle."

I do as I am told.

"You have to dig deeper," he says, "way below the anger,

the hurt, the self-pity.

The pursuit of a dream will heal you. Do this and you

could have wings of an eagle."

But how could an eagle with broken wings ever fly?

Like the wingbeats of a bird, I find strength when I move.

I box.

I swing.

I shoot hoops and miss.

Too small, too shy, too weak.

Instead, I run—

away from bullies who fling racist words like arrows.

Away from my broken heart.

Through the prairie grasses and over the gullies and gulches,

I feel connected to myself, to my family, and to the earth.

The footsteps of my ancestors rise to meet mine.

At home, sports stories leap from old news clippings
and I trace the rings of the Olympic flag—
linked arm in arm like the Lakota prayer
we are all related.
My thoughts turn with pages where Olympians
Jim Thorpe and Buster Charles
smile from faces that look like mine.
Like mine!

Jim Thorpe Wins
Olympic Gold Medal

When the ancestors call for my father,
the word *orphan* seeps into our home like a shadow.
Five of us are too young to leave the nest.
Sid and Margie, my older siblings, keep us together,
but as we grow, we all must pitch in.
To earn money, I sweep the floor of the grocery store.
Later, I hitch a ride to build grain elevators,
sleeping in wrecked cars,
because rooms aren't available for brown-skinned kids like me.

I run into the arms of Haskell Institute in Kansas,

a boarding school where kids from many Indigenous nations

unpack their stories, cultures, friendships.

I am the second smallest on the high school campus,

but I try out for the track team anyway,

only to be told no.

Too slow!

During summer break, I run and run.

Then I make weights out of cans of concrete

and beg my muscles to grow.

When I return to school, Coach Coffin hands me a team jersey.

Teamwork helps me grow—faster, taller, hopeful,

until I break state high school track records

and hatch a whispery dream. Olympics!

But then . . .
during races,
my arm tingles,
my vision blurs,
my heart pounds.

I am cold and sweaty.

Like a car running out of gas, my energy fades.

What is happening to me?

Coach hands me a spoonful of honey before each race.

It helps so much, I run all the way to a college scholarship.

At the University of Kansas, few students look like me,

and Jim Crow rules linger like a cage of segregation.

No walking on certain streets.

No sharing an apartment with a white teammate.

No joining a fraternity.

Because they are reserved for whites only.

Though friendships blossom on the track team,

Coach Easton is not sympathetic when I weaken and wilt.

Forget the honey—just run, he says.

And I do,

helping the Jayhawks win championships.

But when I tell Coach of my Olympic goal,

he says, *Don't dream too big*,

as if I am not destined to soar.

We are at a championship meet far from Kansas
when I am named an All-American runner—
an honor awarded to the best college athletes in the country.
A photographer calls for an All-American photo.
Then he points at me.
"Hey, you," he says, "the dark-skinned one.
We want you out of the picture."
And, just like that,
my wings are clipped—
a lone bird falling from the sky.

Back at my hotel room, I am swept into currents of sorrow.

My strength is gone for the races I run,

because others see nothing but my race.

Then a memory flickers: the circle my father drew in the dirt.

Wings of an eagle.

The pursuit of a dream will heal you, I hear him say.

I reach for my journal and write down my dream.

Olympic gold medal: 10,000-meter race.

Believe. Believe. Believe!

But my power still drains when it matters most,
and I don't qualify for the 1960 Olympic team.
I graduate from college, marry my sweetheart, Patricia,
and join the US Marines.
The Marine coach wants me to train for the 1964 Olympics,
after I see a doctor about my body's mystery.
Diagnoses: hypoglycemia and borderline diabetes.
Doc says the proteins and sugars in my body
are out of balance.
The Marines' mantra becomes my own—
Adapt and Overcome.

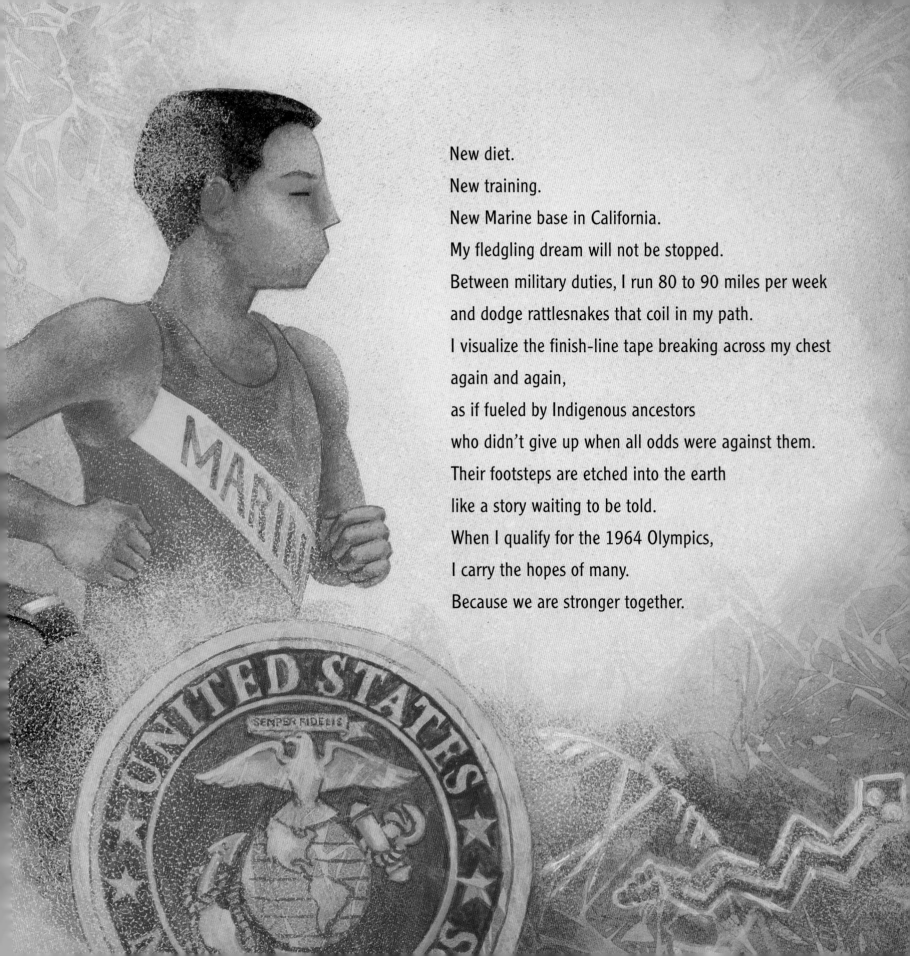

New diet.

New training.

New Marine base in California.

My fledgling dream will not be stopped.

Between military duties, I run 80 to 90 miles per week

and dodge rattlesnakes that coil in my path.

I visualize the finish-line tape breaking across my chest

again and again,

as if fueled by Indigenous ancestors

who didn't give up when all odds were against them.

Their footsteps are etched into the earth

like a story waiting to be told.

When I qualify for the 1964 Olympics,

I carry the hopes of many.

Because we are stronger together.

October 1964—Olympic Village, Tokyo

Borrowed shoes carry me to Tokyo's Olympic Village,

where new track spikes are promised to USA Olympians

by a shoe company with a big name

but with no promise for me.

"There are only enough for medal contenders," the salesman says.

"I'm going to win," I declare.

Nobody expects me to win.

Jim Thorpe is the only Indigenous athlete

to have won Olympic gold in track and field.

And no American has ever won the Olympic 10,000-meter race.

Ever!

The man's snickers drive me to another shoe vendor

who hears what happened and hands me spikes

to replace the ragged threads on my feet.

At my hotel room, apologies and more shoes arrive.

When the starting gun fires,

I am ready to fly.

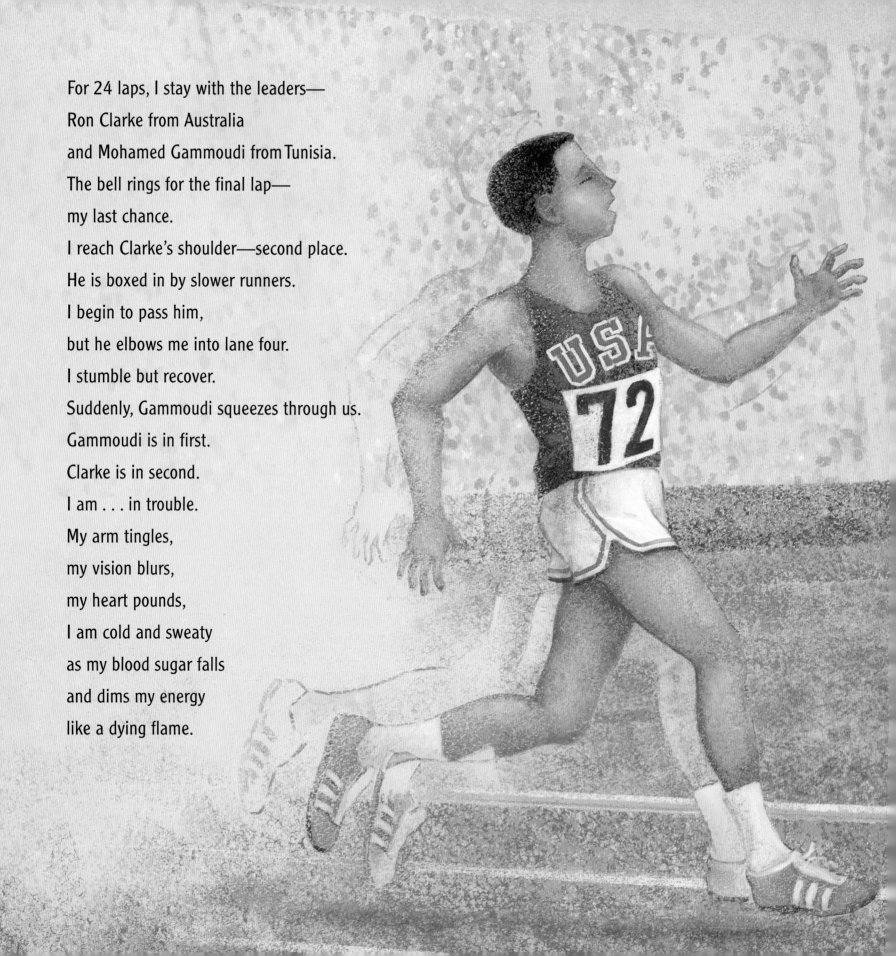

For 24 laps, I stay with the leaders—
Ron Clarke from Australia
and Mohamed Gammoudi from Tunisia.
The bell rings for the final lap—
my last chance.
I reach Clarke's shoulder—second place.
He is boxed in by slower runners.
I begin to pass him,
but he elbows me into lane four.
I stumble but recover.
Suddenly, Gammoudi squeezes through us.
Gammoudi is in first.
Clarke is in second.
I am . . . in trouble.
My arm tingles,
my vision blurs,
my heart pounds,
I am cold and sweaty
as my blood sugar falls
and dims my energy
like a dying flame.

My hope is nearly snuffed out

until I pass a slower runner.

Was that an eagle on his jersey?

Wings of an eagle! Surely it is a sign!

Believe, believe, believe!

The footsteps of my ancestors now thunder through my own.

In a final kick,

I raise my knees, pump my arms, stretch my stride, and then . . .

I shoot forward like there are wings on my feet.

My chest breaks through the tape.

I win gold!

I search for that slower runner and find . . .
there is no eagle on his jersey.
But as the American anthem plays,
and the gold medal slides over my head,
I feel the brush of an eagle's wings on my spirit,
and my own footprints become
part of the story to be told.
That's when I imagine my father's voice:

You can step out of the circle now, son.

On Pine Ridge Reservation,
an eagle feather headdress,
fit for a warrior,
is placed on my head.
I am given a Lakota name, Tamakoce Te'hila,
which means "Respects the Earth" and "Loves His Country."
There are songs and drums and dances in my honor.
Now it is my turn to plan a Giveaway—
to share my thanks and blessings,
and to spread the wings of others.

**Because we are stronger together
when we link arms with all people.**

BILLY'S GIVEAWAY

Billy has devoted much of his life to helping people, improving the lives of Indigenous communities, and inspiring others to be of service.

In 1986, Billy cofounded Running Strong for American Indian Youth, a nonprofit organization that supports the needs of Indigenous communities, with Eugene L. Krizek of Christian Relief Services.

Access to water. Running Strong's Mni Wiconi program connects reservation homes to running water so that residents don't have to carry water from creeks for drinking, cooking, and bathing.

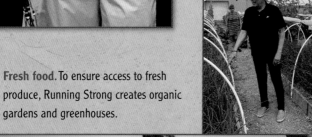

Critical needs. Running Strong provides critical needs like food, school supplies, and winter clothes for those in need.

Fresh food. To ensure access to fresh produce, Running Strong creates organic gardens and greenhouses.

Heat. To combat brutal winters, Running Strong helps struggling families pay their heating bills through the Heat Match program.

Community enrichment. Running Strong creates community centers with space to play, socialize, and take classes.

Supporting dreams. Running Strong's Dreamstarter program supports the dreams of Native youth through financial support, mentorship, networking, and media.

Supporting culture. Running Strong partners with schools, cultural societies, youth camps, and museums for enrichment programs to promote Lakota language and culture.

A NOTE FROM BILLY MILLS

Dear Reader,

I want to share with you the words that have empowered me and influenced my footprints laid on Mother Earth from the time of my mother's passing to this very day. *"You have to dig deeper—way below the anger, the hurt, the self-pity. The pursuit of a dream will heal you. Do this and you could have wings of an eagle."*

When I was young and felt heartache from the unbearable grief of losing my mother—as well as from bullying, poverty, and racism—these words from my father gave me direction and confidence. With clarity of mind, I could make positive decisions in the face of hopelessness. There were moments when I wanted to give up on life because it felt unfair, unjust, and cruel. I stumbled many times on my path, but I did not quit. Looking back, I now know that the choices I make on my journey are what define my destiny.

My father's words also challenged me to take the values, traditions, and spirituality of my culture and place them into my everyday life. As I ran on lands once occupied by Native ancestors, I felt their presence guiding me with the Lakota values of fortitude, courage, humility, wisdom, responsibility, and generosity. And as I stood on the Olympic podium, having won a gold medal against all odds, I felt that I had been

> **YOU HAVE TO DIG DEEPER—
> WAY BELOW THE ANGER,
> THE HURT, THE SELF-PITY.
> THE PURSUIT OF A DREAM WILL HEAL YOU.
> DO THIS AND YOU COULD HAVE
> WINGS OF AN EAGLE.**

given a gift by Wakan Tanka (the Creator). I was proud of my accomplishment, but the real reward was knowing that, by not giving up, I honored myself, my Oyate (tribal nation), the United States, and my tiwahe (family).

In Lakota culture, if you receive good fortune, it is tradition to share it with your community. In time, my wife, Pat, and I realized that my Olympian status could help Lakota and other Indigenous communities around the world—many of which struggle with poverty, health challenges, unemployment, and basic needs. That mission became my Giveaway, beginning with

> **IF YOU DEVELOP YOUR SKILLS
> TO EQUAL YOUR PASSION
> AND BRING THEM TOGETHER,
> MAGIC CAN HAPPEN.**

cofounding the charitable organization Running Strong for American Indian Youth. Centering my Giveaway around Lakota values honors Indigenous people who endure today despite centuries of unimaginable traumas and injustices. I have learned that being helpful is the greatest reward.

I hope my story inspires you to follow an interest that grows into a passion. As my father told me, our passions are what sustain us. When passion meets skills or talent, magic happens, and over time your magical creations just may be looked upon as a miracle. While you chase your own dream with determination and hard work, be a compassionate citizen of the world. Embrace your culture, honor the past, and use your voice and your choices to create a hopeful future. Strive for global unity through the dignity, character, and beauty of diversity. Finding common ground through the similarities of our virtues and values has taught me and my friends from around the world that we are all related, and together we can soar as if we all had wings of an eagle.

Your friend through reading,
BILLY MILLS, Tamakoce Te'hila (Loves His Country)
Oglala Lakota (Sioux) Tribal Nation

A NOTE FROM S. D. NELSON

Dear Reader,

Billy Mills is my hero. I have an old photo of him as a teenager in his Haskell track uniform (which you can see on the next page) posted near my drafting table, where I look at it every day. It is a reminder of my younger years, too. Billy inspired me as a young man because in some ways I saw my own life reflected in his. It is his journey, the process of striving for a goal, that I admire most about Billy's epic adventure, and I hope you enjoyed reading his true-life story as much as I did illustrating it.

In the early 1950s, the roads on our Standing Rock Reservation were mostly dirt and gravel. My grandma Josephine's house was a stucco log cabin. Electricity had been installed for light bulbs and a radio. There was no running water, so the toilet was an outhouse in the backyard and we kids took our baths in a washtub in the woodshed. I attended my first powwow at age five on the old rodeo grounds outside the town of Fort Yates in 1955. I remember clinging tightly to my dad's trouser leg as I witnessed an extraordinary spectacle—people gathered in a great circle, a chorus of singers chanting like howling coyotes, pounding drums stirring my blood. In the center of the great ring, men danced about: Some were dressed in wolf skins, one man wore deer antlers and pranced about as though he had four legs, and another crouched low to the ground, turning with outstretched eagle wings. He was soaring—flying! Before my very eyes, people had become animal spirits.

Like Billy, I understood at a young age the transformative power of the animal spirits. As a boy, my mother told me traditional stories about Coyote, the Trickster, and Iktómi, the Spider. I learned that the stars were the spirits of my ancestors, that my great-great-grandfather Maȟpíya Kiny'An (Flying Cloud) still rode his snorting horse along the White Road of the Milky Way. Mom said if I looked carefully, I would see the Great Bear and the Star That Did Not Turn—the North Star. She told me the Life Force, or the Great Mystery, is named Wakan Tanka, that all of creation—the four-legged beings, the tall standing trees, even the wind—has a spirit and is alive.

In Billy's story we see how these spirits and those of the ancestors influenced his journey, and they influenced my artistic path as well. My illustrations offer a contemporary interpretation of Lakota ledger-style artwork that originated in the late 1800s. Traditionally, my Lakota people painted on animal skins, but with the coming of the European Americans, their hunting ways drastically ended. They turned to paper to create their art. Living near US forts—many even imprisoned in them—they had access to discarded ledger books filled with lists of merchandise and numbers. The used record books had served the tradesmen's purpose and were headed for the trash heap. Instead, Native men used them as a surface on which to create images of their vanishing culture. On this lined paper, they drew stylized figures in hard outlines filled with color. Human and animal figures are typically drawn in profile with very simplified facial features.

Ironically, and in a visually striking manner, the intentions of the bookkeeper and the Indian artist remain separate—like oil on water. The Indian's images seem to float atop the lined paper of the white man with its strange written words and numbers. Sadly, and in the most compelling way, the two cultures never seem to connect. In many ways that disconnection continues today.

So, dear reader, although my Native people have suffered great trauma, we are recovering and we will not remain brokenhearted. For the sake of our children, we remember the past, but we bury our bitterness. Our Indigenous people extend the hand of friendship. Today, we stand with the strong hearts and determination of our ancestors. We remember and honor the come-from-behind kick of Billy Mills in the 1964 Olympic Games and his enduring Warrior Spirit.

We lace up our shoes and get in the game!

Your friend through reading,
S. D. NELSON, *Maȟpíya Kiny'An (Flying Cloud),*
Hunkpapa Lakota—Standing Rock Sioux Tribe

Drawing done in the traditional ledger style on lined paper by S. D. Nelson.

MORE ABOUT BILLY MILLS

from Donna Janell Bowman

In 2015, I stumbled upon a brief mention of Billy Mills and was immediately inspired to learn more about him and about the Native American culture and history that shaped him. I immersed myself in at least one hundred articles about Billy, in addition to scores of print and filmed interviews, and countless viewings of the 1964 broadcast footage of his Olympic win. To better understand Lakota and Native American history, I read many books, listened to oral histories, and watched multiple documentaries. But the most valuable and treasured part of my journey was meeting Billy in person and launching an ongoing collaboration.

William "Billy" Mervin Mills was born on June 30, 1938, the third youngest of twelve children born to Sidney and Grace Mills, though several earlier siblings died young. On poverty-stricken Pine Ridge Reservation, Billy's sizable family (which also included a half sibling and an orphaned cousin) did not own a car, and their dilapidated house did not have running water, indoor plumbing, air-conditioning, or enough coal for consistent winter heat. Billy's father worked various jobs when he could, but there was never enough money. Thankfully, Billy's grandfather had a garden and cattle ranch that kept the family fed. When his beloved sister Estella contracted tuberculosis, and later his mother developed cancer and tuberculosis, a second modest home was added across the street.

Billy's father, Sidney Sr., was a mentor who exposed him to Lakota storytellers, culture, language, and spirituality. From him, Billy learned to live life as a warrior, which means using the virtues of fortitude, humility, respect, generosity, honor, bravery, wisdom, and compassion. Billy absorbed

At age 16 in a Haskell Institute yearbook photo.

I WAS RUNNING IN SEARCH OF MY IDENTITY. I WAS RUNNING TO FIND BILLY.

tales of his ancestors, such as his grandfather who was a child with the band of Oglala war leader Crazy Horse when they surrendered in 1877 to US troops at Red Cloud Agency, near Fort Robinson, Nebraska. As an amateur boxer and sports fan, Sidney encouraged his son to identify and chase a dream, perhaps in sports. But racism and oppression would prove to be Billy's greatest life obstacles. While on Pine Ridge Reservation, Billy was often teased because he wasn't 100 percent Lakota. Off the reservation, he was bullied because he was Native American. He never knew where he fit in.

Once orphaned and at risk of falling into dangerous habits, Billy chose to attend Haskell Institute—a residential Indian high school in Lawrence, Kansas. Surrounded by a diverse Indigenous population, Billy felt accepted and sheltered from the outside world. Haskell was evolving from a shameful history of assimilation. Assimilation began in the mid-1800s and involved taking children away from their Indigenous families, cultures, traditions, and languages and placing them in Indian boarding schools, where they were forced to adopt the ways of white American society. Many schools ruled with cruelty and persisted with their assimilation goals until the 1960s. By the time Billy enrolled as a Haskell student in the 1950s, enrollment there was voluntary, cruelty was no longer acceptable, and assimilation goals were waning. The Haskell athletics coach, Tony Coffin, encouraged Billy's love of running, and he was a much-needed fatherly influence. As Billy says, all you need is for one person to believe in you.

Billy was a good student at the University of Kansas, but the severity of racism and legal segregation—a national problem—limited his rights and freedoms, and he often suffered verbal and physical abuse. Despair almost led Billy to end his own life. He chose instead to focus on his athletic goal. He says, "I was running from rejection, from being orphaned. . . . The Indians called me mixed blood; the white world called me Indian. I was running in search of my identity. I was running to find Billy."

As a proud US Marine, Billy almost missed his Olympic chance. Some Marine athletes, hoping to qualify for the US Olympic team, were invited to participate in elite training at California's Camp Pendleton, but Billy wasn't—until he forcefully argued that he could make the Olympic team if the Marine Corps would believe in him. Fortunately, they gave him a chance. During this time, Billy received the diagnoses of hypoglycemia and borderline diabetes, serious conditions that affect the body's natural blood sugar, organ function, and moods. Almost sixty years later, Billy's diagnoses were changed to hypoglycemia and insulinoma, a tumor on his pancreas that he has likely had for most of his life. The condition causes excess insulin and other symptoms similar to diabetes.

Heading into the Olympic 10,000-meter race, all odds were on the 1960 Olympic gold medalist from the Soviet Union and the world record holder from Australia. Ultimately, Billy bested his own personal record by a staggering 46 seconds and set an Olympic record. One week after his win in the 10,000-meter, he also placed fourteenth in the Olympic marathon. In 1964, the only other American athlete to have medaled in the 10,000-meter was Louis Tewanima, a Native American athlete from the Hopi Tribe who earned the silver medal in 1912. As of this writing, the only other Native American athlete to win Olympic gold in a track and field event was Jim Thorpe in 1912.

In 1965, Billy set a new world record in the 6-mile event at the National Amateur Athletic Union Track and Field Championship. In 1968, Billy qualified for the Olympic trials, but he was caught in the middle of an ongoing conflict between the Olympic Committee and the African American–led Olympic Project for Human Rights, and was ultimately not allowed to run the 5,000-meter qualifying race. Instead, he joined Jesse Owens at the Olympics as a liaison between US athletes and the US Olympic Committee. Billy ended his athletic career shortly thereafter and eventually worked in insurance and then with the Bureau of Indian Affairs.

In 1986, he cofounded the charitable organization Running Strong for American Indian Youth as his lifelong Giveaway. Its stated mission is to help "Native American people meet their immediate survival needs—food, water, and shelter—while implementing and supporting programs designed to create opportunities for self-sufficiency and self-esteem." The organization has raised millions of dollars for the improvement of Indigenous communities in thirty states and dozens of tribal nations.

Billy Mills has been inducted into many Halls of Fame for his athletic achievements, and he has been recognized for his tireless work toward equality and social justice. He is most proud to have been honored by the Anti-Defamation League for his efforts in combating hate, and to have been awarded the Presidential Citizens Medal, presented by President Barack Obama, in recognition of Running Strong's humanitarian contributions.

Crossing the finish line to win gold at the 1964 Olympics.

For many years, Billy has traveled the world speaking about diversity and empowerment, and enlightening audiences about the generational trauma and poverty caused by nineteenth-century colonialism and western expansion. He teaches about the long-term consequences of this country's Manifest Destiny—its determination to seize all lands between the

ALL YOU NEED IS FOR ONE PERSON TO BELIEVE IN YOU.

Atlantic and Pacific Oceans, regardless of existing occupants—and the fifteenth-century Doctrine of Discovery, decrees by the Catholic Church that encouraged the seizure and colonization of any lands not inhabited by Christians, notably Indigenous people. (In 2023, Pope Francis formally repudiated the validity of such doctrines.) Today, researchers often refer to the mass destruction of Native people and their way of life as a cultural holocaust.

But Billy also reminds audiences that the Lakota people around the United States, like other Native American people, are resilient and talented. They are community leaders, physicians, teachers, engineers, artists, business owners, athletes, actors, musicians, and more. The Lakota culture is alive and well, and the Lakota language is rebounding in schools and communities. Billy Mills's story is a reminder that we are all shaped by our environment, our culture, and the triumphs and traumas of our ancestors. But we each have dreams to chase and a world to make better. Especially if we all live the Lakota prayer *we are all related*.

Billy and his wife, Patricia, an acclaimed artist, are blessed with four daughters and many grandchildren and great-grandchildren. I am immensely honored to have collaborated on this true story with Billy and Pat. They welcomed me into their home, their lives, and their memories. Through hours of conversation, smiles, and even a few tears, this book took shape, and my heart swelled. I hope all readers who meet Billy in these pages open their minds and hearts, too.

You can learn more about Billy Mills and Running Strong for American Indian Youth at indianyouth.org.

KEY DATES AND SELECT ACHIEVEMENTS

1938 Born on Pine Ridge Reservation, South Dakota, on June 30

1953–57 Attends Haskell Institute in Kansas; cross-country champion three years in a row

1956–57 Two-time state mile champion in track and field. Ranked fourth in nation as a senior.

1957–62 Attends University of Kansas

1959–61
- Three-time National Collegiate Athletic Association Cross Country First Team All-American
- USA Amateur Athletic Union Men's All-American Track and Field Team

1962 Graduates with Bachelor of Science degree in education, University of Kansas

1962–65 Attends US Marine Officer Candidate School and is commissioned as a second lieutenant, eventually rising to the rank of captain

1964 Wins Olympic gold medal in the 10,000-meter event with a time of 28:24.4, setting a new Olympic record and a new USA record; places fourteenth in the Olympic marathon with a time of 2:22:55.4

1965 Sets four track and field records:
- World record in the six-mile event with a time of 27:11.6
- Breaks his own US record in the 10,000-meter event with a time of 28:17.6
- US indoor record in the 3,000-meter event with a time of 7:56.4
- US indoor record in the three-mile event with a time of 13:25.4

1968 Qualifies for the 1968 Olympic trials with the fastest time in the 5,000-meter event but is not allowed to compete in the finals because of a technicality while racial tension between the US Olympic Committee and African American athletes escalates

1979–80 Member of President Jimmy Carter's Council on Physical Fitness and Sports

1983 Subject of the semibiographical movie *Running Brave*

1986 Cofounder and national spokesperson of Running Strong for American Indian Youth

1990 Named Healthy American Fitness Leader by President George H. W. Bush's Council on Sports, Fitness & Nutrition

1995 Receives Jackie Robinson Humanitarian Award, United States Sports Academy; testifies in front of the US Senate about issues faced by Native Americans

2000 Named *Sports Illustrated* Athlete of the Century for South Dakota

2003 Cofounds Billy Mills Running Strong for American Indian Youth Scholarship, University of Kansas

2012 Receives Presidential Citizens Medal from President Barack Obama

2014 Receives Acts of Courage Award, Anti-Defamation League; receives the National Collegiate Athletic Association's highest honor, the Theodore Roosevelt Award

2015 Receives the President's Council on Physical Fitness and Sports Lifetime Achievement Award

Lifetime Inducted into numerous Halls of Fame, including the USA Track and Field Hall of Fame and the US Olympic Track & Field Hall of Fame